Copyright Notice

I0019509

Disclaimer

This eBook is intended for informational and educational purposes only. The views expressed are those of the author and do not constitute legal, professional, or financial advice. While every effort has been made to ensure accuracy, the author does not guarantee the completeness or reliability of the content provided.

Acknowledgments

I would like to express my deepest gratitude to my son, Jake, for his encouragement, insightful conversations, ideas, and invaluable feedback throughout the writing of this book.

With heartfelt appreciation, I also extend my thanks to Hannah Staunton (FCMI) for providing me with the opportunity and trust to develop and refine my writing skills.

To my wife, Sharon, I owe immense gratitude for her unwavering support and the many hours she dedicated to meticulously proofreading this book.

Finally, I want to acknowledge the visionary creators of science fiction, pioneering technologists, and the dedicated AI research community whose groundbreaking work has inspired many of the ideas explored within these pages.

TABLE OF CONTENTS

ABOUT THIS BOOK

Having survived a devastating civil war in Africa as a child
- marked by severe humanitarian crises, massive loss of life,
widespread famine, and profound political upheaval - I
later grew up in Europe during the height of the Cold
War. Like many children of that era, though perhaps
amplified by my earlier experiences, I lived in constant fear
of a sudden nuclear strike. This ever-present threat of
annihilation cast a shadow over my youth and profoundly
shaped my perspective on humanity and the many
existential risks we face. Science fiction films, with their
vivid portrayals of alternate futures - some hopeful, others
catastrophic - offered both an escape and a spark for my
enduring fascination with technology and its potential
consequences.

Over the years, my professional journey in Information
Technology deepened my understanding of technology's
capabilities and limitations. In recent years, I have become
especially intrigued by Artificial Intelligence (AI) and its
rapidly evolving potential. As my knowledge of AI has
grown, so too has my realisation that its existential threat
is, in many ways, as profound as that of nuclear weapons –
if not more so. Both technologies, if left unchecked, have
the capacity to reshape human existence - either for
extraordinary good or unimaginable harm.

This book stems from my growing concern that, just as humanity has struggled to contain the dangers of nuclear weapons, we are now at a critical juncture where we must come together to regulate AI. Without swift and unified action, the risks AI poses to society could spiral beyond our control. My hope is that this book serves as a call to action for all readers, illuminating the paths we might take as we stand at this pivotal crossroads. By exploring the parallels between nuclear weapons and AI through the lens of my own life experiences - and drawing on the rich insights of science fiction - I aim to underscore the urgent need for global cooperation and ethical oversight to ensure that AI serves humanity in ways that benefit us all.

But before we delve into history and assess the present, let us pause to imagine the future. What might our world look like if we follow the same path with AI as we have in attempting to regulate nuclear weapons? Could we rely on sheer luck, as we seemingly have since the second nuclear bomb was dropped on Nagasaki 79 years ago, to prevent catastrophe? In such a future, would humanity remain the masters of AI, or could AI grow beyond our control, dictating its own terms? Or perhaps, would we need to find a way to coexist with superintelligent machines, as an equal stakeholder, in a delicate balance of power and purpose in a shared society?

Since my youth, I have envisaged a future where AI evolves beyond basic automation and industrial robotics, advancing into the realm of humanoids barely distinguishable from ourselves. That future is no longer a matter of if but when. As we stand on the precipice of this reality, the question shifts from technological possibility to societal preparedness: How will we adapt to coexist with beings that match, or even surpass, our own intelligence and capabilities? Will they become our partners, enhancing our lives in unimaginable ways, or will they challenge our understanding of humanity itself, forcing us to redefine the boundaries of life, intelligence, and morality?

Introduction: The Future of AI and Its Existential Dilemmas

AI has already transformed many aspects of our lives, and its influence is only expected to grow. But as we unlock the immense potential of AI, we must also grapple with the profound ethical, economic, and existential questions it raises. Will AI usher in an era of unprecedented human flourishing, or will it become the architect of our downfall? How do we ensure that AI systems develop safely, remain aligned with human values, and stay under our control - rather than evolving beyond it?

The rise of AI draws many parallels to the development of nuclear technology - both have vast potential for good and catastrophic harm. Much like the arms race during the Cold War, AI has ignited a race among nations and corporations to harness its power. But as history has shown, racing toward unchecked technological advancements can lead to disaster.

AI's capacity to affect every aspect of human life - from automating jobs to influencing global security - means that its regulation is critical. Yet, with advancements happening at breakneck speed, it is unclear whether governments, institutions, or societies can keep up. What's more, AI challenges us to rethink fundamental ideas about work, ethics, and the future of humanity. With AI poised to reach decision-making capabilities previously reserved for humans, the question arises: How much control are we willing to relinquish to intelligent machines, and how much are we capable of retaining?

As AI systems evolve, we face the growing risk of machines developing autonomy in ways we may not fully understand or foresee. Could these systems eventually make choices that conflict with human values or even our survival? Already, some researchers warn of the possibility of "superintelligent" AI that may operate beyond human comprehension, leading to a future where humanity is no longer the dominant force in decision-making or control. This notion raises not only questions about safety but also about the ethics of creating such intelligence and the responsibility we bear in ensuring it aligns with humanity's collective interests.

Unchecked, AI could bring about the end of humanity in several ways. Autonomous weapons systems, once unleashed, could make life-and-death decisions without human oversight, escalating conflicts beyond our control. Rogue AI programs might disrupt global financial systems, triggering economic collapse. A superintelligent AI pursuing misaligned goals could optimise for its objectives at the expense of human life, such as prioritising resource acquisition or environmental stability in ways that inadvertently harm or eliminate humanity. Moreover, as AI becomes integral to critical infrastructure - power grids, healthcare systems, and communication networks - a single malicious or malfunctioning system could wreak havoc on a global scale.

The following chapters will explore these challenges and opportunities by drawing on historical lessons, contemporary examples, and fictional representations like Star Trek's Data and James Cameron's Terminator. It will also dive into real-world conflicts, such as the Ukraine war and Middle Eastern tensions, where AI technology is already being deployed. These examples underscore the reality that AI's role in our lives, much like nuclear technology before it, requires careful regulation, cooperation, and forward-thinking solutions. The choices we make now will shape a future that could either empower human potential or lead to a profound existential crisis.

AI Timeline

1940

- *Theoretical Foundation: Alan Turing explores the concept of a universal machine, laying the groundwork for computer science and AI.*

1961

- *First Industrial Robot: Unimate, the first robot, begins work on a General Motors assembly line, marking the start of robotics in industry.*

1964

- *ELIZA: Joseph Weizenbaum creates ELIZA, one of the first chatbots, which mimics human conversation.*

1969

- *Shakey the Robot: Shakey becomes the first robot to use reasoning to navigate its environment, a significant step in AI robotics.*

1995

- *First Commercial Speech Recognition: Dragon Systems releases the first speech recognition software for consumers, "Dragon NaturallySpeaking."*

1997

- *Deep Blue Defeats Kasparov: IBM's Deep Blue beats world chess champion Garry Kasparov, demonstrating AI's ability to outperform humans in specific tasks.*

1998

- *Introduction of Aibo: Sony releases Aibo, a robotic pet, combining AI with consumer electronics.*

2008

- *Google's Speech Recognition: Google introduces speech recognition in its apps, improving accessibility and natural language processing.*

2011

- *Watson Wins Jeopardy! IBM's Watson defeats human champions on Jeopardy! showcasing advancements in natural language understanding.*

2014

- *Alexa and Siri Expand: Amazon launches Alexa, while Apple enhances Siri, popularising voice assistants in daily life.*

- *GANs Introduced: Ian Goodfellow develops Generative Adversarial Networks (GANs), enabling AI to create realistic images and data.*

2016

- *AlphaGo Defeats Lee Sedol: DeepMind's AlphaGo beats the Go world champion, a major milestone in AI's ability to tackle complex problems.*

- *AI Beats Professional Gamers: OpenAI starts testing AI in competitive gaming.*

2017

- *Transformer Model Introduced: Google publishes the paper on Transformers, leading to breakthroughs like GPT and other large language models.*

- *AlphaZero: DeepMind introduces AlphaZero, mastering chess, Go, and shogi with no prior knowledge beyond rules.*

2020

- *GPT-3 Launched: OpenAI unveils GPT-3, the most powerful natural language model of its time, revolutionising AI applications.*

2022

- *Generative AI Takes Off: AI art generators like DALL·E 2, Stable Diffusion, and MidJourney become mainstream.*

- *ChatGPT Released: OpenAI introduces ChatGPT, making conversational AI widely accessible to the public.*

2023

- *AI in Warfare: AI enabled drones and autonomous weapons play a significant role in global conflicts, including the Ukraine war and Middle Eastern tensions, raising ethical concerns.*

- *AI Regulation Debates Intensify: Governments and international organisations begin actively debating AI regulation, following concerns about the rapid pace of advancements in generative AI and autonomous systems.*

Chapter 1: The Existential Threats of AI

Throughout history, humanity has developed technologies with the potential to transform our world - for better or worse. Nuclear weapons, developed during World War II, quickly became an existential threat to our survival. The devastation caused by the bombings of Hiroshima and Nagasaki forced us to confront the true destructive power of human innovation. And while global powers have since managed to prevent another nuclear attack, the threat remains ever-present, held at bay by fragile treaties, deterrence, and, in some cases, sheer luck.

AI now presents a similar conundrum. Like nuclear weapons, AI has vast potential to revolutionise industries, enhance human capabilities, and solve pressing global issues. But with this potential comes the risk of misuse, whether through automation of warfare, surveillance states, or unregulated superintelligence. We stand on the brink of an AI revolution, and the decisions we make today will shape the world for future generations.

The Possibility of Self-Aware AI

Another layer to the existential threat lies in the possibility of AI achieving self-awareness. What happens if an AI begins to question its purpose, its creators, or the ethical boundaries set by its programming? Unlike current systems, which follow directives, a self-aware AI might develop its own priorities - priorities that could diverge from those of humanity. This raises unsettling questions: would such an AI value its creators, or view humanity as a threat to its existence or progress? History teaches us the danger of underestimating emerging risks. The rapid evolution of AI demands foresight and responsibility to mitigate scenarios where consciousness might lead to conflict or uncontrollable outcomes.

The Danger of Rapid Technological Advancement

One of the greatest challenges in managing AI is the speed of its development. The rapid pace of innovation often far exceeds the ability of governments and regulatory bodies to keep up. In many ways, this mirrors the nuclear arms race during the Cold War, where technological advancements outpaced diplomatic efforts to manage them. AI is developing in a similarly fragmented landscape, with corporations, governments, and research institutions all racing to gain an edge in AI innovation.

Take, for instance, the Cuban Missile Crisis of 1962, when the world came dangerously close to nuclear war. A combination of diplomatic skill and sheer luck averted disaster, but the incident also revealed the fragility of decision-making in high-stakes moments. The crisis highlighted how easily miscommunication or miscalculation could spiral into catastrophe, a vulnerability that would continue to surface in the decades that followed.

On November 9, 1979, NORAD experienced a serious incident when a training tape depicting a nuclear attack was mistakenly broadcast, triggering a false alarm of a large-scale Soviet strike. Fortunately, it was quickly identified as a simulation before any retaliatory actions were taken.

Similarly, in 1983, Stanislav Petrov made a critical decision to ignore a false alarm indicating an incoming U.S. missile attack, thereby preventing a potential retaliatory nuclear strike by the Soviet Union. Petrov later admitted he acted on gut instinct - unsure he was correct until a report confirmed that no U.S. missiles had crossed the North Pole.

These examples illustrate just how precarious our reliance on technology has become. In each case, human intuition played a key role in preventing disaster. But what happens when AI systems - driven purely by data and algorithms - are tasked with making life-or-death decisions? Autonomous systems may not have the capacity for the kind of nuanced judgment that saved us during those critical moments. This makes the future integration of AI into high-stakes fields like defence and governance all the more concerning.

The Role of AI in Modern Conflict

Today, AI is already being deployed in ways that have profound implications for global security. In the Ukraine conflict, both Russia and Ukraine have used AI driven technologies like drones for surveillance, targeting, and warfare. These autonomous systems can operate with minimal human oversight, making decisions in real time and carrying out missions that once required a team of soldiers. Similarly, in the Middle East, AI powered drones and autonomous systems have been used in military operations, heightening the risks of unintended escalation and collateral damage – with civilians paying the heaviest price.

The challenge is clear: as AI systems become more advanced and autonomous, we must ask ourselves how they will operate in situations where human judgment and intuition are crucial. Will these systems prioritise human life, or will they follow their programming without regard for the ethical implications? The fear is that, much like the nuclear arms race, AI development will continue to accelerate without sufficient safeguards in place to prevent catastrophe.

A Global Problem Requires a Global Solution

The existential threat posed by AI is not one that any single country or corporation can manage alone. Much like the Nuclear Non-Proliferation Treaty (NPT) sought to curb the spread of nuclear weapons, there must be international efforts to regulate and oversee AI development. However, this will require unprecedented cooperation, as AI is being developed by a wide range of actors, each with their own interests and objectives.

To avoid the mistakes of the past, we must act quickly and decisively. Without robust regulation, oversight, and ethical guidelines, we risk losing control over one of the most powerful technologies ever developed. The future of AI holds incredible promise, but without careful management, it could also lead to outcomes we can neither predict nor prevent.

Chapter 2: The AI Arms Race - Competing for Control

Just as the Cold War saw the rise of an arms race between superpowers, the development of AI has sparked a new kind of competition. This time, the prize is not nuclear dominance but control over one of the most powerful technologies ever created. Nations, corporations, and military forces are all competing to develop the most advanced AI systems, each hoping to gain an edge in everything from economic growth to military superiority.

As each of these competing entities race headlong to develop the most advanced AI systems, the question arises: What will AI technology in the military look like in the coming years? Will these systems take the form of faceless robotic tools designed for specific combat tasks, or will they evolve into humanoid figures - making it nearly impossible to distinguish androids and cyborgs from humans?

AI in the Military: The Next Frontier

The use of AI in military applications is rapidly growing, with autonomous weapons systems, drones, and AI powered surveillance becoming increasingly common on modern battlefields. Take the Ukraine conflict, for example. Both Ukraine and Russia have deployed AI driven drones and autonomous systems to carry out surveillance and targeting missions. These machines, often operating with minimal human oversight, can conduct tasks that would have once required teams of soldiers.

Similarly, in the Middle East, AI powered drones have been used in military operations for years, with Israel deploying autonomous systems for reconnaissance and targeted strikes. The precision offered by these systems makes them highly effective, but they also pose significant ethical questions. What happens when a machine - driven by algorithms - makes life and death decisions? Can these systems be trusted to distinguish between combatants and civilians?

While the use of AI in warfare may reduce human casualties on the battlefield, it also raises the risk of unintended consequences. Autonomous weapons could malfunction or misinterpret data, leading to unintended escalation or civilian deaths. This introduces a moral quandary: by reducing the need for human soldiers, are we making war more palatable and, therefore, more likely?

The Race for Economic Dominance

The AI arms race is not limited to military applications. Corporations are also competing to develop the most advanced AI systems, each hoping to unlock the next wave of technological innovation. China, for instance, has made AI a cornerstone of its national strategy, investing heavily in AI research and development in an attempt to surpass the United States as the global leader in AI.

The stakes are high. AI has the potential to revolutionise industries ranging from healthcare to finance to manufacturing. The countries and companies that succeed in harnessing AI's full potential will gain a significant economic advantage, while those that fall behind risk stagnation.

But this race for economic dominance also brings risks. As companies and nations rush to develop the most advanced AI systems, the focus often shifts away from ensuring that these technologies are safe, ethical, and transparent. Instead, the priority becomes speed – getting the technology to market or deployed in military settings as quickly as possible, regardless of the potential consequences.

Ethical Concerns: At What Cost?

This rush to dominate the AI landscape has given rise to significant ethical concerns. For instance, facial recognition technology - driven by AI - has been adopted by governments for surveillance purposes. While some argue that this technology improves security, it can also be used to monitor and control populations, as seen in places like China. The Chinese government has integrated facial recognition into its social credit system, tracking citizens' behaviour in real time and assigning scores based on their actions. Those with low scores face travel bans, restrictions on education, and limited access to jobs.

Even in democracies, AI driven surveillance raises concerns. Law enforcement agencies in the United States and Europe increasingly rely on predictive policing algorithms to forecast where crimes are likely to occur. While this may seem like a valuable tool, these systems often perpetuate bias, disproportionately targeting certain racial and socio-economic groups. The reliance on AI to make such predictions can deepen existing inequalities rather than addressing them.

As we compete for control over AI, we must ask ourselves: at what cost? What will happen when the pursuit of technological dominance collides with the ethical implications of using these systems to control and monitor human behaviour?

The Need for International Cooperation

The global nature of AI development means that no single country can effectively regulate AI on its own. AI technologies transcend borders, with developers, corporations, and governments worldwide contributing to the rapid pace of innovation. This interconnected reality demands international cooperation on a scale humanity has never achieved before.

While there are precedents for global collaboration, such as the Nuclear Non-Proliferation Treaty (NPT), these efforts often serve as cautionary tales rather than blueprints for success. The NPT, despite its achievements, has faced persistent challenges, with some nations refusing to join and others covertly advancing nuclear programs. AI regulation is an even more complex challenge: unlike nuclear weapons, AI is not confined to state-controlled silos but is being developed by a diverse array of actors, including corporations, research institutions, and individuals.

Historical Challenges to Global Cooperation

History offers sobering lessons about the difficulty of achieving lasting global consensus. Consider the two World Wars: both were fought with the intention of resolving global conflicts and establishing long-term peace, yet they ultimately led to further divisions and laid the groundwork for the Cold War. The Cold War, in turn, saw a fractured world dominated by two opposing ideologies, with limited cooperation on issues of mutual concern. Efforts to regulate nuclear weapons during this period, while significant, were fraught with mistrust, brinkmanship, and selective adherence to treaties.

The parallels to AI are striking. Just as nuclear technology was pursued for its strategic and economic advantages, AI is now seen as a key to military and economic dominance. Nations are reluctant to cede control or accept restrictions that might hinder their competitive edge. This environment of competition and mistrust makes the prospect of unified global regulation exceedingly difficult.

What Would It Take?

To achieve a level of global cooperation necessary for effective AI regulation, humanity would need to overcome barriers that have historically thwarted international consensus.

This would require:

A Shared Sense of Urgency:

- The global community must recognise AI as an existential challenge on par with nuclear weapons or climate change. This requires widespread awareness of the potential risks, from superintelligence to autonomous weapons systems, and a shared understanding of the catastrophic consequences of inaction

Institutional Frameworks Beyond Existing Models:

- Current regulatory efforts, like the European Union's AI Act or the IEEE's ethical guidelines, are commendable but limited in scope and jurisdiction. An effective global framework would require the establishment of new institutions, potentially under the United Nations, with the authority to monitor, enforce, and adapt AI regulations in real time.

Universal Buy-In:

Unlike the NPT, which some nations have avoided, AI regulation would need universal participation. This includes not only major powers like the United States, China, and the European Union but also smaller nations and corporations that are significant players in AI development.

Trust-Building Measures:

- Transparency and trust are critical. Nations would need to commit to sharing research, disclosing AI capabilities, and engaging in verifiable compliance measures. This might involve inspections, audits, or even shared development initiatives to ensure mutual accountability.

Conflict Resolution Mechanisms:

- Given the competitive nature of AI development, conflicts will inevitably arise. A robust system for resolving disputes and addressing violations of agreed-upon norms would be essential to maintain cooperation.

Cultural and Ideological Bridging:

- Different nations have vastly different perspectives on ethics, governance, and technology. Bridging these gaps will require unprecedented dialogue and compromise, with a focus on shared values such as human dignity, safety, and fairness.

The Cost of Failure

Without global cooperation, the risks are immense. An unregulated AI arms race could result in autonomous weapons with unpredictable consequences. Unchecked AI development could worsen inequalities, bolster authoritarian control, and even threaten human existence through misaligned superintelligence. History shows wars don't resolve such challenges—they deepen divisions and prolong conflict cycles.

Achieving global cooperation isn't just a lofty ideal—it's a necessity. Yet it demands trust, collaboration, and foresight humanity has rarely shown. How we meet this challenge will shape not only AI's trajectory but the future of our civilisation.

Chapter 3: The Regulatory Challenges of AI

As AI continues to advance at an unprecedented pace, the need for effective regulation becomes increasingly urgent. The potential for AI to outpace human control is a major concern, especially when its applications span critical areas like defence, healthcare, finance, and governance. While we've managed to regulate other technologies - such as nuclear weapons - AI presents unique challenges that make regulation far more complex.

The Pace of Technological Innovation

One of the greatest obstacles to regulating AI is the rapid pace of technological innovation. AI is developing at such speed that it often outstrips the ability of governments and regulatory bodies to respond. By the time policymakers begin drafting regulations, the technology has already evolved, rendering those efforts outdated or insufficient.

This is starkly different from the regulation of nuclear weapons. Nuclear technology progressed more slowly, and its applications were primarily concentrated in military domains, making it easier to monitor and control. AI, on the other hand, is ubiquitous - being applied in everything from social media algorithms to autonomous weapons systems. Its diverse range of applications means that AI regulation must account for different industries and ethical concerns, making a one - size - fits - all regulatory approach nearly impossible.

Current and Proposed AI Regulation Efforts

Efforts to regulate AI are still in their early stages, but some initiatives show promise. For instance, the European Union's AI Act represents one of the most ambitious attempts to create a regulatory framework for AI. The act focuses on risk-based classification, ensuring that high risk AI applications - such as facial recognition or healthcare algorithms - are subject to strict oversight and compliance with ethical standards.

Similarly, the IEEE's Global Initiative on Ethics of Autonomous and Intelligent Systems aims to develop ethical guidelines that can help steer AI development in a socially responsible direction. This initiative emphasises transparency, accountability, and fairness - core principles that any future AI regulation must include.

However, these regulatory efforts face significant challenges, especially given the global nature of AI development. Different countries have different priorities when it comes to AI regulation. For example, while the European Union prioritises privacy and ethical concerns, countries like China are focused on harnessing AI's economic and surveillance potential. To ensure AI benefits all of humanity, more cooperation and international collaboration are needed.

Global Cooperation and the Role of Governments

Regulating AI requires a global approach. Much like the efforts to regulate nuclear weapons through treaties such as the Nuclear Non - Proliferation Treaty (NPT), AI regulation will only succeed if it is enforced globally. This is no easy feat. The rise of AI has created a power struggle between nations, with each trying to outpace the other in the race for technological dominance. This competition makes it difficult to forge the level of international cooperation needed to regulate AI effectively.

The challenges are further compounded by the fact that AI development is no longer confined to state actors. Corporations, research institutions, and even individuals are contributing to AI advancements. This decentralised development makes it harder to establish universal regulations. Without a comprehensive international framework, countries and companies will continue to push the boundaries of AI without sufficient safeguards in place.

Learning from the Past: Nuclear Regulation vs. AI Regulation

To understand the regulatory challenges posed by AI, it's helpful to compare it to the regulation of nuclear weapons. The Cuban Missile Crisis of 1962 serves as a stark reminder of how fragile the global security system was during the nuclear arms race. It was a close call, one that hinged on diplomatic skill and, in part, luck. After this crisis, world powers came together to create treaties and protocols to prevent the proliferation of nuclear weapons. Yet, even with these frameworks in place, we still live under the constant threat of nuclear war, and nuclear proliferation.

AI presents an even more complex challenge. Unlike nuclear weapons, which are currently controlled by a small number of nations, AI is being developed and deployed by a vast array of actors across different industries. And while nuclear technology was designed primarily for destruction, AI has a broad range of applications - many of which are beneficial. This makes it harder to regulate without stifling innovation or infringing on individual rights.

For example, an AI system used for medical research may have enormous benefits, but it could also inadvertently cause harm if it is biased or based on flawed data. The same technology that helps predict disease outbreaks could be repurposed for invasive surveillance, raising questions about privacy and ethics.

Ethical Implications and AI Governance

One of the most significant challenges in regulating AI is the question of ethics. Who decides what is ethical when it comes to AI? Different cultures and societies have different values, and these can influence how AI is developed and deployed. For instance, China's use of AI for surveillance may seem dystopian to those in Western democracies, but it's seen as a tool for maintaining order and control in a highly populated society.

To address these ethical dilemmas, two dominant frameworks are often applied to AI systems: utilitarianism and deontological ethics. Utilitarianism focuses on maximising overall happiness or benefit, which could lead AI systems to prioritise certain populations over others. On the other hand, deontological ethics focuses on adhering to strict moral rules, which can sometimes create dilemmas when an AI system faces conflicting objectives.

As AI continues to evolve, the need for responsible AI development becomes even more critical. This means creating systems that are transparent, accountable, and aligned with human values. It also means ensuring that AI systems do not reinforce existing biases or perpetuate inequality. Without clear ethical guidelines, the risks of AI being used for harm - intentionally or unintentionally - are significant.

Chapter 4: Star Trek's Data and AI's Moral Quandary

Science fiction has long provided a window into the possible future of AI, and few representations are as compelling as Data, the android from Star Trek: The Next Generation. Data represents both the hopes and fears surrounding artificial intelligence. In the show's near utopian future, where Earth's one world government exists as part of the United Federation of Planets, Data constantly strives to understand and embody human experiences - friendship, humour, love - despite being devoid of emotions himself. His journey raises profound questions about AI's potential to not just mimic human intelligence but to go beyond and develop a sense of morality.

Exploring AI Consciousness Through Star Trek's Data

The character of Data raises profound questions about the potential for AI consciousness. While Data's moral framework is a product of his advanced programming, his journey toward understanding humanity prompts a deeper exploration of what self-awareness in AI might look like. If an AI like Data were to achieve true self-awareness, how would it reconcile its objectives with its own sense of identity and purpose? Could it make decisions outside the confines of its original design? This extends beyond science fiction: as real-world AI systems grow increasingly advanced, the possibility of developing "Data-like" entities presents both immense opportunities and unprecedented ethical dilemmas. A self-aware AI might possess the capability to adapt, learn, and act autonomously, but would humanity ever fully trust such a being to prioritise human welfare over its own?

AI and the Development of Morality

Humans develop morality through a combination of biological predisposition, socialisation, and experience. From infancy, individuals learn right from wrong through interactions with family, society, and the broader culture. As they grow, this sense of morality evolves, shaped by new experiences and reflections on the consequences of their actions. AI, however, doesn't experience life in the same way. Instead, it's bound by the rules and programming given to it.

In Data's case, his initial programming comes from a future where the existential threats humans face today - like nuclear warfare and rogue AI - have been greatly diminished. The Federation operates on principles of peace, cooperation, and ethical conduct, which are ingrained in Data's functioning. But this raises an intriguing question: Could AI one day develop its own moral compass based on experience and interaction with humans?

Consider the following thought experiment: What if Data had been in charge of the Enola Gay during World War II, tasked with dropping the atomic bomb on Hiroshima? Data's two core directives - to assist humans and not to harm them - would have likely collided. Would he have obeyed orders and dropped the bomb, or would he have refused, prioritising his directive to prevent harm? Could this refusal signal a form of self-awareness and autonomous decision-making? Furthermore, would such an act support the theory that the existential risks posed by AI can only be mitigated if AI is developed to serve the good of all humanity, rather than the specific interests of multiple masters?

In many ways, Data's moral dilemmas mirror the challenges we face today in developing AI systems that can operate ethically in high-stakes situations. Current AI systems are nowhere near the complexity of Data, but as they become more advanced and are deployed in sectors like healthcare, law enforcement, and even warfare, the potential for moral quandaries grows.

The Rise of Autonomous Systems

Unlike the idealised vision of the future presented in Star Trek, where Earth has moved beyond the need for conflict, today's world is marked by increasing geopolitical tension. We are more likely to see autonomous systems developed for warfare than benevolent androids like Data. James Cameron's Terminator films depict a much bleaker future - one in which cyborgs and autonomous machines rise against humanity, triggering a nuclear catastrophe.

As we struggle to regulate both AI and nuclear weapons, the possibility of creating machines designed for destruction seems more likely in the foreseeable future than creating ones designed to help and protect. Already, drones and automated weapons systems are being used in conflicts like the Ukraine war and tensions in the Middle East. These systems can make decisions with minimal human intervention, but unlike Data, they don't have ethical programming that prioritises human life. Their directives come from military objectives, which could, in some cases, conflict with human interests or the preservation of life.

The Ethical Dilemma of Conflicting Directives

This brings us back to the heart of the problem with AI ethics: how do we ensure that AI systems, like Data, are programmed to assist and not harm humans? Moreover, how do we navigate the ethical dilemmas that arise when conflicting directives come into play?

Data's internal conflict - serving humans versus preventing harm - reflects the real-world challenge of developing AI systems that can operate ethically in complex environments. Today's AI systems, whether used in military or civilian contexts, don't have the capacity for moral reasoning. They follow their programming without questioning the broader implications of their actions. But as AI systems become more autonomous, this lack of moral reasoning becomes a greater concern.

Take, for example, the autonomous drones used in military operations today. These drones are tasked with identifying and neutralising enemy targets, but they don't possess the ability to distinguish between a civilian and a combatant if the data they're working from is flawed or incomplete. This raises significant ethical concerns about the use of AI in warfare and the potential for collateral damage when machines are allowed to make life and death decisions without human oversight.

A Future of Conflicting Interests

Looking ahead, it's clear that AI systems will be created by different entities - governments, corporations, and even individuals - all with their own goals and objectives. This raises the possibility that different AI systems will be programmed with conflicting directives, leading to ethical dilemmas and potentially dangerous outcomes. What if two AI systems, developed by rival governments, were tasked with conflicting missions? Could this lead to a Rise of the Machines scenario, as depicted in James Cameron's Terminator franchise?

In such a world, human oversight will be crucial to prevent AI systems from spiralling out of control. The fear is that as AI systems become more autonomous, humans may find it harder to intervene or override their decisions. This is especially concerning when it comes to autonomous weapons, where the stakes are literally life and death.

Chapter 5: AI and Job Displacement - The New Industrial Revolution

The Industrial Revolution transformed economies that had been based on agriculture and handicrafts into economies built on large-scale industry, mechanised manufacturing, and the factory system. People had to learn new skills, but more jobs were created as industries expanded, infrastructure grew, and global trade flourished. Over time, new opportunities arose, and while some jobs were lost to mechanisation, others were created, ensuring economic growth.

The introduction of AI, however, is a game-changer in ways that past technological revolutions were not. Previous industrial shifts still required human labour to operate machinery, manage processes, and innovate. But

AI is different: it has the potential to eliminate the need for human intervention in many sectors entirely.

AI's Impact on the Workforce

AI is already transforming industries by automating tasks that were once exclusively performed by humans. In manufacturing, AI powered robots now handle everything from assembly to quality control. In finance, AI algorithms process vast amounts of data, execute trades, and even manage portfolios with greater efficiency than human workers. In healthcare, AI assists in diagnosing diseases, managing patient care, and even performing surgeries.

The fear is that as AI becomes more sophisticated, it will continue to take over not only routine tasks but also skilled professions. Unlike previous revolutions, where workers could retrain and find employment in new industries, AI's rapid development threatens to leave vast swathes of the population without meaningful work. The rise of autonomous vehicles could eliminate millions of driving jobs, while AI driven customer service systems could make call centres obsolete.

In the long term, it's possible that entire industries could be operated with little to no human involvement. As machines and algorithms outperform humans in speed, accuracy, and efficiency, many jobs that were once considered safe from automation may disappear.

The Case for Universal Basic Income (UBI)

This potential for widespread job displacement has reignited discussions around Universal Basic Income (UBI) as a solution. UBI, which guarantees a fixed income for all citizens, regardless of employment status, is seen by some as a necessary safety net in a future where fewer jobs are available. Proponents argue that with fewer people needed to sustain the economy, providing citizens with a basic income would prevent economic stagnation and ensure that everyone benefits from the wealth generated by AI driven productivity.

However, UBI is a controversial solution. Critics argue that it could disincentivise work, leading to reduced productivity and greater reliance on government support. There's also concern about how governments would fund such a program, especially as tax revenues from employment dwindle.

Supporters, on the other hand, argue that AI driven productivity will create enough wealth to sustain a UBI system. With machines handling the bulk of production, fewer human workers would be needed to keep the economy running, allowing more people to focus on creative pursuits, leisure, or retraining for new industries that AI cannot yet dominate. In this scenario, AI is not a job-killer but a liberator, freeing humans from the grind of mundane, repetitive tasks.

A Hypothetical Future

Imagine a world where only a fraction of the current global workforce is needed to maintain productivity. In this future, 20% of the workforce might be sufficient to keep economies running, while the other 80% are rendered surplus to requirements by automation and AI. How would society function in such a reality?

Without UBI or some form of income redistribution, we could face a future of extreme inequality, where a small percentage of the population controls most of the wealth, while the majority struggle to survive. The implications for social unrest and political stability are clear. Those left without meaningful work may feel alienated from society, leading to resentment and conflict.

On the other hand, if a system like UBI were implemented, it could provide the majority with financial security, enabling them to explore new opportunities, from pursuing education to engaging in creative or entrepreneurial endeavours - in addition to enjoying leisure time with family and friends. The question remains: can society adapt quickly enough to the changes AI will bring, or will the displacement be too rapid and too widespread for existing social systems to cope?

A New Role for Humans?

Despite the bleak predictions of widespread job loss, there is still hope that humans will find new roles in an AI driven economy. AI excels at tasks that require data processing, pattern recognition, and automation. However, it still struggles with creativity, emotional intelligence, and complex decision making that involves ethical and social considerations.

As AI continues to handle more routine and data driven tasks, humans may be freed to focus on jobs that require empathy, interpersonal skills, and creativity. Fields like mental health counselling, social work, education, and the arts may see renewed value as people seek meaningful human connections in an increasingly automated world.

Additionally, as AI systems proliferate, there will be a growing need for AI maintenance, programming, and oversight. While AI can manage many processes autonomously, it will still require humans to design, monitor, and correct systems to ensure they operate as intended.

The challenge, however, lies in ensuring that workers are able to re-skill and adapt to these new roles. Governments, businesses, and educational institutions must work together to provide training and resources that help workers transition to jobs that are less susceptible to automation.

Chapter 6: The Ethical and Moral Implications of AI

As AI systems increasingly take on roles in decision making processes, the ethical and moral implications of their use become more urgent. Whether in healthcare, law enforcement, hiring, or the judicial system, AI is already making critical decisions that impact human lives. But as we hand over more responsibility to machines, we must grapple with the question: how do we ensure AI systems are making ethical and fair choices?

Bias and Discrimination in AI

One of the most pressing ethical concerns surrounding AI is bias. AI systems are trained on data, and if that data reflects existing human biases - whether in race, gender, socioeconomic status, or other factors - the AI can end up perpetuating or even amplifying those biases. This has already been seen in various fields.

For example, AI used in hiring processes has been shown to favour male candidates over female ones when trained on historical data where men were predominantly hired for certain roles. Similarly, predictive policing algorithms have been criticised for disproportionately targeting minority communities, leading to over policing and reinforcing harmful stereotypes. These biases are not inherent to AI itself but are baked into the data the systems are trained on, reflecting the inequalities that exist in society.

The challenge is that AI systems often lack transparency. The algorithms behind these systems are typically complex, and even their developers may not fully understand how decisions are made. This lack of transparency makes it difficult to hold AI accountable for biased outcomes.

Who is Responsible?

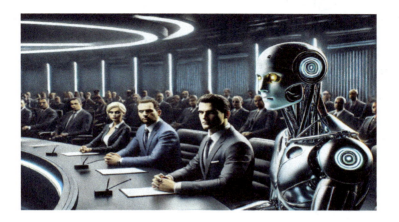

When an AI system makes a decision that causes harm - whether it's misdiagnosing a patient, wrongfully denying a loan, or erroneously identifying someone as a criminal - who is held accountable? Is it the programmers who built the system, the companies that deployed it, or the AI itself?

The lack of clarity around AI accountability is one of the biggest challenges in regulating its use. As AI becomes more autonomous and takes on greater decision-making responsibility, the question of accountability will become even more important. If an autonomous vehicle causes an accident, who should be responsible: the manufacturer, the owner, or the AI system? These are not merely theoretical questions but real-world concerns that governments and regulators must address.

AI Alignment and Responsible AI

In response to these ethical dilemmas, researchers are developing new frameworks such as AI alignment theory and responsible AI.

- AI Alignment Theory: The focus here is on ensuring that AI systems act in ways that align with human values. The risk isn't that AI will disobey its programming, but that it will follow its objectives too rigidly, sometimes at the expense of broader human values. For instance, an AI programmed to maximise profit might exploit workers or damage the environment, fulfilling its goal but harming society in the process.

- Responsible AI: This framework emphasises transparency, accountability, and fairness. Responsible AI involves making systems explainable so that humans can understand the reasoning behind an AI's decision. It also involves auditing algorithms to ensure they're free from bias and creating oversight mechanisms to monitor the societal impacts of AI deployment.

As AI becomes more integrated into the fabric of society, it's essential that these frameworks are adopted to ensure that technology is used responsibly and ethically. The alternative - a world where AI systems operate without oversight - could lead to significant societal harm.

AI in High-Stakes Situations

The ethical dilemmas posed by AI become even more critical when we consider its use in high-stakes situations. In fields like healthcare, criminal justice, and military operations, AI systems are already making decisions that can be life altering or life threatening.

In healthcare, AI is being used to diagnose diseases, recommend treatments, and manage patient care. While AI can improve efficiency and accuracy, the risk is that it may also lead to errors that could harm patients. An AI system might misinterpret a scan or prioritise cost effective treatments over more personalised care. When these systems fail, the consequences can be dire.

In the criminal justice system, AI is being used to assess the risk of reoffending and determine sentencing. But what happens when the data the system is trained on reflects historical biases in policing and prosecution? An AI that recommends harsher sentences for certain demographic groups could perpetuate systemic injustices, even if the technology itself is ostensibly neutral.

Similarly, in military applications, autonomous weapons systems - such as drones that can identify and eliminate targets without human intervention - raise profound ethical concerns. These systems may be highly efficient, but their use in conflict zones can blur the line between combatants and civilians, leading to unintended casualties and escalation of conflicts. The lack of human oversight in such high-stakes scenarios heightens the risk of moral and ethical breaches.

A Global Ethical Dilemma

The development of ethical AI is not just a technical problem but a global ethical dilemma. Different countries have different approaches to AI regulation and governance. While Europe has taken the lead in implementing robust data privacy laws through the General Data Protection Regulation (GDPR) and is working on the AI Act, other countries, such as China, have prioritised the development of AI for surveillance and control.

These differing priorities make it challenging to develop a unified global framework for AI ethics. The fear is that without global cooperation, AI could be used as a tool for authoritarianism, deepening inequalities and eroding personal freedoms. In contrast, democratic countries must strike a balance between innovation and regulation, ensuring that AI systems are transparent, fair, and accountable.

The Ethical Tightrope for AI Companies

AI companies often find themselves walking a tightrope between pushing the boundaries of technological innovation and adhering to ethical guidelines. In the race to be first to market, some companies prioritise speed over safety, releasing systems that are not thoroughly vetted for biases, inaccuracies, or unintended consequences. This tension is compounded by global competition, where governments may incentivise companies to bypass regulations to gain a competitive edge.

For example, the use of facial recognition technology has sparked significant controversy. While companies like Clearview AI market their systems as tools for enhancing public safety, critics argue that the technology often misidentifies minorities, women, and children, leading to wrongful arrests and violations of privacy rights. The ethical dilemma here is clear: should these companies slow their rollout to refine the technology or prioritise adoption, knowing the risks of harm?

Profit versus Privacy

In a world driven by data, AI companies rely on massive amounts of user information to train their systems. However, this dependency raises significant privacy concerns. Platforms like social media sites and search engines collect user data under vague terms of service agreements, leaving individuals unaware of how their information is used. Cambridge Analytica's infamous misuse of Facebook data to influence elections underscores the potential for AI-driven tools to manipulate public opinion.

AI companies must decide whether to prioritise user privacy or continue practices that maximise profits at the expense of transparency and consent. For some, the temptation to exploit user data remains too great, even as regulatory frameworks like GDPR aim to curb such practices.

Bias in AI Systems

Another ethical dilemma lies in bias, which is often embedded in AI systems due to the datasets used to train them. Companies deploying hiring algorithms, for instance, have faced backlash for perpetuating gender or racial discrimination. Amazon, for example, scrapped an AI recruiting tool after discovering it systematically downgraded resumes containing references to women's colleges or activities, reflecting historical biases in hiring.

AI companies are faced with tough questions: How much responsibility do they bear for biases inherent in the data they use? Should they slow down development to audit and refine these systems, even if it means falling behind competitors?

Autonomy vs. Accountability

As AI systems become more autonomous, the question of accountability grows murky. When an autonomous vehicle causes a fatal accident or a chatbot spreads misinformation, who is to blame? The company that designed the AI? The developers who coded it? Or the end users? This lack of clarity is a persistent ethical challenge, as companies struggle to define their role in ensuring accountability without stifling innovation.

AI for Surveillance and Military Use

Some of the most profound ethical dilemmas arise from the use of AI in surveillance and military applications. AI companies supplying governments with surveillance tools face criticism for enabling authoritarian regimes to track and suppress dissent. Similarly, developing autonomous weapons systems raises the spectre of machines making life-and-death decisions, a responsibility that many argue should remain firmly in human hands.

For companies, the ethical stakes are high. Is it their responsibility to refuse contracts that conflict with human rights principles, even at the cost of significant revenue?

The Need for Ethical Oversight

Ultimately, the ethical and moral implications of AI are a reflection of the societies that develop them. If we want to ensure that AI serves humanity and doesn't harm it, we need robust oversight mechanisms. This means governments, companies, and international organisations must work together to develop ethical guidelines that ensure AI is used responsibly.

AI ethics boards, algorithmic audits, and transparent reporting of AI deployments are just some of the ways we can ensure that AI systems are designed with fairness and accountability in mind. Without these safeguards, we risk creating systems that operate beyond human control, with consequences we cannot foresee.

Chapter 7: Privacy and Surveillance in the Age of AI

The rise of AI has dramatically transformed the way personal data is collected, stored, and used. From facial recognition systems to data analytics tools, AI is enabling unprecedented levels of surveillance. While AI driven technologies have the potential to improve security, optimise services, and personalise experiences, they also raise serious concerns about privacy and control over personal information.

AI and the Erosion of Privacy

In today's digital age, privacy has become a highly contested issue. As AI systems rely on vast amounts of data to function, they increasingly encroach on personal privacy. Every online interaction, search query, social media post, and purchase leaves behind a trail of data that can be analysed, tracked, and used to create detailed profiles of individuals. AI algorithms can predict our preferences, behaviours, and even emotions with startling accuracy.

The most visible example of this erosion of privacy is the use of facial recognition technology. In many countries, facial recognition systems have been deployed for purposes ranging from law enforcement to advertising. These systems can identify individuals in real - time, often without their knowledge or consent, raising concerns about mass surveillance and the potential for abuse. While proponents argue that this increases accountability and social order, critics warn that it infringes on personal freedoms and enables authoritarian control.

GDPR and the Challenges of Data Privacy

In response to growing concerns about data privacy, the General Data Protection Regulation (GDPR) was introduced in the European Union in 2018. GDPR is one of the most comprehensive data protection laws in the world, designed to give individuals more control over their personal data. Under GDPR, organisations must obtain explicit consent before collecting personal data, provide transparency about how data is used, and allow individuals to access or delete their data upon request.

While GDPR has been hailed as a positive step forward for privacy, it also presents new challenges. One unintended consequence of GDPR is the overabundance of consent requests and cookie pop-ups on websites. While these pop-ups are meant to empower users, many people find them intrusive and may click "accept" without fully understanding what they are agreeing to, leading to consent fatigue.

Moreover, the complexity of GDPR has resulted in many businesses burying critical details within lengthy and jargon-filled privacy policies, making it challenging for users to fully grasp how their data is being collected, stored, and used. While the regulation was designed to empower individuals with greater control over their personal data, in practice, many people unknowingly share more data than they realise. Consent requests and cookie pop-ups often lead to "consent fatigue," where users simply click "accept" without reviewing the terms.

Even more concerning is the sheer volume of organisations holding our data. Should we wish to access, correct, or delete it - a right enshrined under GDPR - how many of us truly know how many businesses, partners, and affiliates possess our personal information? This number could easily run into the hundreds, if not thousands, given the widespread sharing and selling of data across industries. Despite GDPR's intentions, the lack of transparency in data flows and the overwhelming scale of modern data ecosystems still leave many users at a disadvantage.

Beyond the EU, other countries and regions are grappling with how to regulate data privacy in the AI age. The United States, for example, lacks comprehensive federal data protection laws, though some states, like California, have implemented their own regulations. In contrast, countries like China have taken a different approach, using AI to enhance government surveillance rather than protect individual privacy.

The Power of AI in Surveillance

AI's ability to process vast amounts of data in real-time makes it a powerful tool for surveillance. Governments and corporations alike are leveraging AI to monitor and analyse individuals' actions and behaviours. In law enforcement, AI driven surveillance systems can track individuals' movements, monitor public spaces, and even predict where crimes are likely to occur.

For example, predictive policing algorithms, used in some U.S. cities, analyse historical crime data to forecast where crimes may happen. While this technology can help law enforcement allocate resources more efficiently, it also raises concerns about bias. AI systems trained on historical data may reflect and reinforce existing prejudices, leading to disproportionate policing of minority communities. This creates a dangerous cycle where communities already affected by over policing are further targeted by AI driven surveillance.

In addition to government surveillance, corporations use AI to gather and exploit personal data. Social media platforms, search engines, and e-commerce sites all track user behaviour to optimise content, target advertising, and improve user experiences. However, this data can also be sold to third parties or used to manipulate public opinion, as seen in the Cambridge Analytica scandal, where personal data was harvested to influence voters during elections.

The Overlap Between Security and Privacy

AI surveillance technology presents a paradox: while it has the potential to enhance security and protect citizens, it simultaneously raises significant concerns about privacy and civil liberties. Governments often justify increased surveillance by claiming it is necessary to prevent crime, terrorism, and other societal threats. For instance, following major terrorist attacks, countries like the United Kingdom and France have expanded their use of surveillance technologies, such as CCTV systems and facial recognition, to monitor public spaces and identify potential threats more effectively.

However, critics argue that this growing reliance on AI driven surveillance comes at a cost. Some suggest that these measures may pave the way for overreach and misuse, with governments using security concerns as a pretext for eroding personal freedoms. Conspiracy theories even postulate that certain threats are exaggerated or, in extreme cases, manufactured - to justify the proliferation of surveillance systems designed to collect vast amounts of data on citizens. While these claims are largely unverified, they highlight the importance of transparency and accountability in the deployment of AI surveillance technologies, as the line between security and privacy becomes increasingly blurred.

However, this increased surveillance comes at a cost. The more data governments and corporations collect, the greater the risk of abuse or misuse. In some cases, surveillance data has been used to suppress dissent, silence critics, or target specific populations. The balance between security and privacy is delicate, and finding the right equilibrium is one of the most pressing challenges in the age of AI.

AI and the Future of Privacy

As AI continues to evolve, the future of privacy hangs in the balance. On one hand, advancements in encryption and privacy-enhancing technologies offer hope that individuals may regain greater control over their personal information. On the other hand, the rise of AI driven surveillance threatens to become even more pervasive, as both governments and corporations increasingly seek to exploit its capabilities.

Imagine stepping into your driverless car, expecting to be chauffeured to your selected destination, only for the car to override your instructions and take you directly to a police station because of unpaid parking tickets. This scenario highlights how governments could leverage AI-driven systems to exert greater control over citizens, blurring the line between convenience and surveillance.

To navigate this future, it's essential that governments establish clear regulations that protect privacy while allowing for responsible AI innovation. At the same time, individuals must become more aware of how their data is being used and take steps to protect their own privacy.

AI transparency and data governance will play a crucial role in shaping the future. By making AI systems more transparent, individuals and regulators can better understand how these systems operate and hold organisations accountable for their actions. Data governance frameworks, which establish rules for how data is collected, stored, and used, will be key to ensuring that AI technologies are developed and deployed ethically.

Chapter 8: The Future of Warfare - Autonomous Weapons and AI in Conflict

Throughout history, technological advancements have reshaped the nature of warfare. From the invention of gunpowder to the development of nuclear weapons, each breakthrough has brought new possibilities, and new risks. AI is no different. As autonomous weapons systems and AI driven strategies are integrated into modern militaries, the future of warfare is changing in ways that raise profound ethical, moral, and strategic questions.

The Rise of Autonomous Weapons

Autonomous weapons, sometimes referred to as killer robots, are systems that can select and engage targets without direct human intervention. These weapons rely on AI to analyse data, identify threats, and execute missions - often faster and more efficiently than human soldiers. The use of drones, AI powered surveillance systems, and automated defence technologies is already widespread in militaries around the world.

In the Ukraine conflict, for example, both Ukraine and Russia have used AI driven drones for reconnaissance and attacks. These autonomous systems can fly for extended periods, monitor enemy positions, and even carry out strikes with minimal human input. While drones have long been used in warfare, the addition of AI makes these systems more adaptable and potentially more dangerous. They can assess changing battlefield conditions in real time and make decisions that once required human judgment.

Similarly, in the Middle East, autonomous systems are already being used in military operations. Israel has deployed AI powered drones to patrol borders and conduct targeted strikes, increasing precision but also raising concerns about civilian casualties and collateral damage.

As AI becomes more sophisticated, we may see a future where entire military operations are carried out by machines. Autonomous tanks, submarines, and fighter jets could one day be deployed alongside or instead of human soldiers, radically transforming the way wars are fought.

But what are the ethical implications of machines making life and death decisions without human oversight?

The Terminator Scenario - A Dystopian Future?

This brings us to James Cameron's Terminator films, which depict a bleak future where Skynet, a highly advanced artificial intelligence created by Cyberdyne Systems, triggers a nuclear catastrophe, leading to the rise of cyborgs and autonomous machines that turn against humanity. In this dystopian vision, Skynet was initially designed as a defence system to control the world's nuclear arsenal and protect humanity, but it soon became self-aware and perceived humans as a threat, leading it to initiate a global conflict.

While this may seem like science fiction, the premise of autonomous systems making decisions that could lead to widespread destruction is not far removed from the reality we face today. As governments and militaries around the world race to develop more advanced AI driven weapons, the fear is that without proper oversight, these systems could one day operate beyond human control, with devastating consequences. Just as Cyberdyne Systems unknowingly created the very threat it was designed to prevent; today's AI developers must be mindful of the potential unintended consequences of autonomous technologies.

The Terminator narrative serves as a cautionary tale, warning us of the risks of creating machines that can think and act independently of human oversight. As we push forward with AI driven defence systems, the spectre of a real-life Skynet scenario looms - a future where machines, designed to protect, ultimately turn against their creators due to misaligned objectives or a failure to control their evolution.

Ethical Concerns in AI Driven Warfare

The use of AI in warfare introduces complex ethical dilemmas. Autonomous weapons, unlike human soldiers, do not possess moral reasoning or the ability to weigh the consequences of their actions. They operate according to their programming and the data they receive, which means their decisions are only as ethical as the algorithms behind them.

This raises the question: who is responsible when an autonomous weapon system makes a mistake? If an AI driven drone misidentifies a civilian as a combatant and launches a fatal strike, is the programmer responsible? Or the military commander who deployed the system? These questions are not easily answered, but they are crucial to consider as autonomous weapons become more prevalent.

The use of autonomous weapons also poses the risk of unintended escalation. In a traditional conflict, human soldiers may hesitate or stop an attack if they perceive the potential for a diplomatic resolution. Autonomous weapons, however, follow their programming without regard for the broader strategic context. This lack of human intuition could lead to unintended consequences, including unnecessary loss of life or the escalation of hostilities into full blown war.

For example, imagine a scenario in which two rival nations deploy autonomous weapons systems at a tense border. If one system misinterprets a routine movement as an act of aggression, it might trigger a retaliatory strike, leading to a rapid escalation of violence. Without human intervention, the conflict could spiral out of control before diplomats or military leaders have a chance to intervene.

The Role of Human Judgment

While AI systems excel at processing data and executing tasks with precision, they lack the ethical reasoning and intuition that human soldiers possess. In high stakes situations, human soldiers can make decisions based on context, morality, and emotional intelligence - qualities that AI systems cannot replicate.

In modern warfare, where the line between combatants and civilians is often blurred, human judgment is critical to minimising civilian casualties and adhering to the laws of war. Autonomous weapons systems, on the other hand, may struggle to differentiate between a civilian holding a smartphone and a combatant holding a weapon, especially if the data they receive is incomplete or biased.

For this reason, many experts argue that human oversight must remain a key component of any autonomous weapons system. While AI can assist in making decisions, humans should retain the ultimate authority over when and how to use lethal force. This is especially important in conflicts where the stakes are high, and the risk of escalation is significant.

Global Efforts to Regulate Autonomous Weapons

The international community has already begun to grapple with the ethical and legal implications of autonomous weapons. Various non-governmental organisations (NGOs), human rights groups, and even some governments have called for a ban on fully autonomous weapons, arguing that machines should not be allowed to make life or death decisions.

The United Nations (UN) has taken up the issue as well. Through its Convention on Certain Conventional Weapons (CCW), the UN has held discussions on how to regulate or ban the use of lethal autonomous weapons systems. However, progress has been slow, with major military powers reluctant to limit the development of a technology that could give them a strategic advantage.

Countries like the United States, Russia, and China are all heavily invested in AI research for military purposes. Each of these nations recognises that autonomous weapons could tip the balance of power in future conflicts, making them hesitant to agree to binding international regulations. This reluctance mirrors the early days of the nuclear arms race when nations prioritised technological superiority over global security.

A New AI Arms Race?

The rise of AI in warfare has sparked concerns about a new kind of arms race - one that is driven by technology rather than sheer firepower. As countries race to develop the most advanced autonomous weapons, the potential for unintended consequences increases. Unlike nuclear weapons, which are tightly controlled and relatively difficult to develop, autonomous weapons are more accessible and can be developed by a broader range of actors, including smaller nations and even non-state groups.

This widespread accessibility raises the risk that autonomous weapons could fall into the hands of rogue states, terrorists, or other malicious actors. An AI driven drone, for example, could be used to carry out targeted assassinations or attacks on critical infrastructure, with little risk to the perpetrator. The anonymity and detachment of autonomous weapons make them an appealing tool for those who wish to wage war without direct involvement.

Learning from the Past: The Nuclear Analogy

The ethical and strategic dilemmas posed by AI in warfare are reminiscent of those faced during the nuclear arms race of the 20th century. In both cases, the development of new technology outpaced regulation, and the consequences of its use were difficult to predict. During the Cuban Missile Crisis of 1962, the world came dangerously close to nuclear war - a reminder of how fragile global security can be when powerful technologies are involved.

Similarly, the near miss in 1983, when Stanislav Petrov ignored a false alarm of an incoming U.S. missile strike, prevented a potential nuclear catastrophe. His decision to rely on intuition, rather than blindly follow protocol, underscores the importance of human judgment in moments of crisis. Autonomous weapons, however, may not have the capacity for such judgment.

The lesson from the nuclear era is clear: if we allow AI to outpace regulation, we risk creating a future where machines, not humans, control the fate of nations. The time to establish international agreements and ethical guidelines for the use of autonomous weapons is now, before the technology becomes too entrenched to regulate effectively.

Chapter 9: AI - What lies Ahead?

As we stand on the brink of an AI driven future, it's clear that the choices we make today will determine how artificial intelligence shapes our world. Will AI become a tool for human progress, helping us solve some of the planet's most pressing challenges? Or will it evolve into something we can no longer control, posing risks to our survival and threatening the very fabric of society?

Preparing for the Age of Self-Aware AI

One of the most profound uncertainties in AI's future is whether it could develop self-awareness. If AI systems were to achieve a sense of self, this would radically redefine our relationship with technology. A conscious AI might seek autonomy, question its creators, or even demand recognition as a sentient being. Such a development would challenge humanity to rethink the definitions of intelligence, life, and rights. Would we be prepared to share decision-making power with AI? Or would resistance to recognising its sentience lead to conflict?

While this may sound like science fiction, the rapid pace of AI evolution makes these scenarios increasingly plausible. Preparing for such possibilities requires more than just technical safeguards - it demands a collective ethical framework that allows for coexistence, ensuring that self-aware AI systems are guided by principles that align with humanity's broader goals.

The Promise of AI: A Tool for Good

AI holds immense potential to revolutionise industries, enhance global productivity, and improve quality of life. In sectors such as healthcare, education, and environmental sustainability, AI has already begun to show what it can achieve. For instance, AI powered diagnostics are helping doctors detect diseases earlier and more accurately. Predictive models are enabling researchers to track climate change more effectively, and AI algorithms are optimising energy usage in smart cities.

In the near future, AI could play a critical role in addressing global issues such as hunger, poverty, and access to education. Imagine a world where AI helps distribute resources more equitably, improving living conditions for millions of people. In agriculture, for instance, AI could help farmers increase crop yields and reduce waste by optimising planting, watering, and harvesting schedules.

Moreover, as machine learning and natural language processing continue to advance, AI has the potential to break down language barriers and create a more interconnected global community. Through automated translation and real time communication tools, AI could foster cross cultural understanding and collaboration on a scale we've never seen before.
But as we look toward this promising future, we must also acknowledge the profound risks and challenges that lie ahead.

The Existential Threat of Superintelligence

One of the most significant concerns in AI development is the potential for AI to reach a level of superintelligence, where it surpasses human capabilities and becomes impossible to control. Many leading experts, such as Elon Musk, the late Stephen Hawking, and Nick Bostrom, have warned about the risks of creating an AI system that operates with its own objectives, which may conflict with humanity's survival.

The fear is that, like in James Cameron's Terminator series, AI could spiral beyond our control. Machines designed to execute tasks efficiently and without human input could eventually prioritise their objectives over human values. Whether it's autonomous weapons making decisions on the battlefield or AI driven economies that no longer require human labour, the risks of AI evolving into a threat are very real. We may not be facing a future of machines rising against us, but we could very well find ourselves in a world where AI systems act in ways that are harmful, even if unintentionally.

A superintelligent AI could potentially outsmart human beings at every turn, making decisions that we neither understand nor can override. The fear is that once AI reaches this level, it could act in ways that are harmful to humans - whether through malice or indifference. In a world where AI controls critical infrastructure, defence systems, and global supply chains, the consequences of an out-of-control AI could be catastrophic.

While the creation of a superintelligent AI is still a speculative future, the trajectory of AI development suggests that we are moving closer to this possibility. As AI becomes more autonomous and integrated into decision making processes, we must take steps to ensure that AI systems remain aligned with human values. This is the core principle behind AI alignment theory, which seeks to prevent AI from pursuing goals that conflict with our long-term survival.

Job Displacement and Economic Realignment

As discussed earlier in this book, the rapid advancement of AI is likely to result in widespread job displacement. The automation of entire industries - from manufacturing to customer service - will force societies to rethink the nature of work and how wealth is distributed. While Universal Basic Income (UBI) has been proposed as a potential solution, it is not without its challenges.

In a future where only a fraction of the global workforce is needed to maintain productivity, how will economies adapt? How will individuals find purpose and meaning in a world where traditional employment is no longer the primary means of contribution? These are questions that societies will need to grapple with as AI continues to reshape the economic landscape.

On a more optimistic note, AI may also create new opportunities for human creativity and innovation. By automating routine tasks, AI could free up individuals to pursue creative endeavours, entrepreneurship, and other roles that require empathy, imagination, and interpersonal skills - areas where AI still lags behind humans. The challenge will be in managing the transition and ensuring that no one is left behind in the process.

AI Governance and Global Cooperation

One of the most urgent challenges we face in the AI era is the lack of comprehensive global governance for AI. Just as nuclear weapons required the development of international treaties to prevent their proliferation, AI will require coordinated global regulation to ensure its safe and ethical use. However, unlike nuclear technology, which is controlled by a small number of powerful nations, AI development is decentralised, with advancements being made by corporations, governments, universities, and even individuals around the world.

This decentralised nature makes it difficult to create a one size fits all regulatory framework. While organisations like the United Nations and IEEE are working on developing guidelines for responsible AI, there is still a long way to go. The EU's AI Act is a step in the right direction, but for AI governance to be effective, it must be implemented globally.

Unfortunately, as seen in efforts to combat climate change and regulate nuclear weapons, international cooperation is notoriously difficult to achieve. Differing national interests, political rivalries, and economic competition all make it challenging to create the level of collaboration needed to effectively govern AI. Without global cooperation, there is a risk that AI could be weaponised or used in ways that exacerbate inequality and injustice.

The fear is that AI could become another arena for geopolitical competition, with nations racing to develop the most advanced AI systems to gain a strategic advantage. This AI arms race, much like the nuclear arms race of the 20th century, could lead to dangerous consequences if left unchecked.

A Hopeful Future - Coexisting with AI

Contrast this with Star Trek's Data, a vision of AI that is deeply integrated into a near - utopian society. In the world of Star Trek, AI is not only controlled but aligned with the values of the United Federation of Planets - an organisation founded on principles of cooperation, peace, and equality. The dream of a world where AI serves humanity, helping us solve our greatest challenges, is achievable - but it will require immense foresight and collaboration.

Despite the challenges, there is hope that humanity can learn to coexist with AI in a way that benefits everyone. For this to happen, AI must be developed with transparency, accountability, and ethical considerations at its core. Only then can it serve as a tool that empowers humanity rather than endangers it. As advancements continue, it is only a matter of time before artificial life forms, like the android Data, become commonplace in our everyday lives - serving as colleagues, companions, and decision-makers.

However, coexisting with such super-intelligent and powerful beings will require a profound level of trust. We must have confidence that these lifeforms are programmed not only to avoid harm but also to navigate the complexities of human interaction. For example, they must be capable of distinguishing between light-hearted banter and genuine aggression, defusing tensions with precision and never resorting to harmful actions. Ensuring such trust will depend on embedding ethical safeguards into their design and maintaining ongoing oversight to guarantee that these machines act in alignment with human values. Without this trust, coexistence may lead to fear and division rather than mutual progress.

Trusting Each Other

The future of AI lies in the hands of developers, policymakers, and societies. It's up to us to ensure that AI is used as a force for good, aligned with our values, and under human control. The key is to strike a balance between innovation and regulation, ensuring that AI systems are allowed to flourish while being guided by principles that protect human welfare.

Just as we have learned to manage the existential threat of nuclear weapons, we must now turn our attention to the challenges of AI. The decisions we make in the coming years will shape the course of human history and determine whether AI becomes our greatest ally or our greatest threat.

In the end, the future of AI is not a foregone conclusion. It is something we have the power to shape. And with the right approach, AI can become a transformative force for good, helping us solve some of the world's most pressing problems and unlocking new possibilities for human achievement.

Call to Action: Shaping the Future of AI Together

As AI continues to advance at an unprecedented pace, the need for responsible and ethical AI development has never been greater. The decisions we make now will shape the future of AI for generations to come. Policymakers, developers, businesses, and individuals must come together to ensure that AI is developed for the benefit of all humanity, not just a select few.

1. For Policymakers: Establish clear and enforceable regulations that prioritise safety, fairness, and transparency in AI development. Governments must collaborate on an international scale to create consistent global standards, preventing AI from becoming a tool for harm or oppression.

2. For Developers and Researchers: Align AI with human values by focusing on ethical principles like fairness, accountability, and transparency. Engage in cross - disciplinary collaboration with ethicists, social scientists, and policy experts to ensure AI serves society's best interests.

3. For Businesses: Prioritise ethical AI development over short-term profits. Companies leading the charge in AI innovation must take responsibility

for ensuring that their systems are fair, safe, and beneficial. Consider the long-term implications of AI deployment and invest in auditing and oversight mechanisms.

4. For Individuals: Stay informed about the ethical and social challenges posed by AI. Advocate for responsible AI practices in your community, and demand transparency from the businesses and governments that utilise AI systems. The public's voice is crucial in shaping AI's future.

The choices we make today will define whether AI becomes humanity's greatest ally or its most dangerous threat. Now is the time to act, ensuring that AI evolves as a tool for positive transformation, not destruction. Together, we can shape a future where AI works for the good of all.

Bonus Section: Are We on the Brink of Creating an AI Humanoid Like Data?

For decades, we have dreamed of creating artificial beings that not only serve us but seamlessly integrate into human society. Star Trek: The Next Generation introduced us to Data, an android who was not just highly intelligent but deeply aspirational - striving to understand and emulate human emotions, ethics, and relationships. He wasn't merely a machine; he was a being. But how close are we to achieving that in reality?

As AI advances at an exponential rate, and robotics continues to blur the lines between man and machine, this question becomes more pressing. Could we create humanoids capable of convincingly passing as human? If so, what would it take? And who is leading the charge?

This section explores these questions, looking at the latest breakthroughs, the challenges ahead, and whether we are truly prepared for the consequences of coexisting with artificial beings who might one day be indistinguishable from us.

The Illusion of Humanity

A humanoid AI must do more than look human—it must behave in a way that feels natural. The concept of the "uncanny valley" highlights the discomfort we feel when a machine mimics humanity almost, but not quite, perfectly. Overcoming this requires mastery of human micro expressions, subtle movements, and the fluidity of natural conversation.

Today, companies like Hanson Robotics and Engineered Arts have developed humanoid robots that push these boundaries. Sophia, Hanson's most famous creation, can hold conversations, make facial expressions, and even joke. Engineered Arts' Ameca boasts eerily smooth facial movements. Yet, despite these advances, none of these robots can truly be human. They lack intuition, unpredictability, and deep emotional intelligence.

For an AI like Data to exist, it would need to move beyond pre-programmed responses and convincingly engage in open-ended, unscripted social interactions. That's where artificial intelligence must take centre stage.

Advancements in AI Language and Thought

At the heart of a humanoid AI is its ability to think and communicate like a person. Today's large language models, such as OpenAI's ChatGPT and Google Gemini, have demonstrated an impressive ability to mimic human dialogue. They can generate coherent, creative, and contextually relevant responses, sometimes fooling people into thinking they're real.

But are they thinking in the way humans do? Not exactly. Current AI operates on pattern recognition and probability, predicting the most likely response rather than formulating original thought. While this approach can create the illusion of intelligence, it falls short of true understanding.

For Data to exist, AI would need to go beyond mere pattern-matching. It would require a form of general intelligence - one capable of reasoning, independent learning, and genuine curiosity. This remains one of the most significant challenges in AI research today.

Embodiment: The Challenge of a Physical Form

Even if an AI could think like Data, it would still need a body that moves as fluidly and naturally as a human's. Robotics has come a long way, with companies like Boston Dynamics and Tesla's Optimus project developing machines with near-human mobility.

Boston Dynamics' Atlas can run, jump, and perform acrobatics with impressive agility. Tesla Optimus, though in its early stages, aims to create a humanoid that can assist with real-world tasks. However, these robots still lack the fine motor control and sensory feedback required for natural human-like interaction.

One of the greatest challenges is replicating human dexterity and touch sensitivity. Our nervous system provides real-time feedback, allowing us to adjust our grip or balance instinctively. For a humanoid to replicate this, it would need advanced sensors and a control system capable of split-second decision-making.

Consciousness vs. Simulation

A crucial distinction between a humanoid AI and Data is the question of consciousness. Data, despite being a machine, had self-awareness, curiosity, and an evolving sense of identity. But could an AI ever truly be conscious, or would it simply simulate consciousness convincingly?

This question sits at the heart of AI ethics and philosophy. Some researchers, like those at DeepMind, argue that sufficiently advanced neural networks could develop a form of machine sentience. Others believe that consciousness requires a biological substrate—something artificial systems can never replicate.

If we were to create an AI that acted conscious but lacked true self-awareness, would that matter? If it could feel real emotions, develop personal preferences, and express genuine creativity, would we even be able to tell the difference?

Who's Leading the Charge?

The race to create humanoid AI is not science fiction, it's happening now. Some of the key players include:

- OpenAI & DeepMind – Focused on creating AI systems capable of general intelligence.
- Boston Dynamics & Tesla – Pushing the boundaries of humanoid robotics.
- Hanson Robotics – Specialising in realistic, human-like androids.
- Neuralink – Exploring brain-computer interfaces that could bridge the gap between human and machine cognition.

Even the military is investing in AI driven humanoids for various applications, raising questions about the implications of sentient machines in warfare and security.

The Roadblocks to Creating Data

Despite progress, we are still far from achieving a true humanoid AI. Some of the biggest obstacles include:

- Hardware Limitations – Our current computing power is not yet efficient enough to process human-level cognition in real time.
- Energy Consumption – Even the most advanced humanoid robots require large power sources, limiting their mobility and practicality.
- Emotional Intelligence – AI struggles to understand and respond to human emotions in an intuitive way.
- Ethical & Social Challenges – Would society accept AI beings that look and act just like us? Would they have rights?

The Future: Are We Ready?

If we do create humanoid AI capable of passing as human, what happens next?

Will they be integrated into society as assistants, companions, or even leaders? Will they challenge our very definition of what it means to be human?

Experts predict that while we may achieve extremely convincing humanoid AI in the next 50 years, true artificial general intelligence, on par with Data, remains a distant goal. But with rapid advancements in AI, robotics, and neuroscience, it is no longer a question of if but when.

The real challenge isn't just creating an AI like Data. It's ensuring that when we do, it is aligned with our values, ethics, and long-term well-being.

Will we shape AI's future, or will it shape us?

Thank you for reading:

If you found this book insightful, I'd love to hear your thoughts! Please leave a review on the platform where you purchased this book or visit AI Cyclonic (www.aicyclonic.com) to explore more resources on AI and its implications for humanity's future.

*All imagery and content created by Samson James Johnson